introduction

for countless generations, every Saint David's Day, Welsh schoolchildren don tall black hats in honour of their patron saint riding a dragon down a coal mine or something. But what is done with the hats for the remaining 364¼ days of the year?

The following list of uses has been meticulously researched and collated from folk history and oral tradition by Hen Het* Huw Aaron.

* 'Old Hat', a title signifying respect and absolute reliability.

<u>bin</u>

disguise

cornet

st.ool

Saucepan

<u>child</u>
<u>restraint</u>

<u>step</u>

bucket

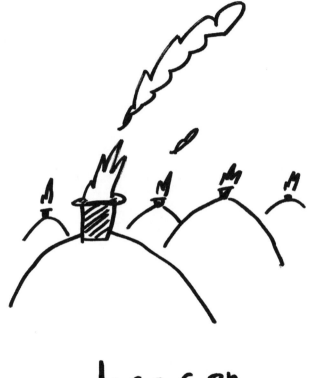

beacon

BBQ

<u>p</u> o <u>t t y</u>

Sack

catcher's mitt

candle

gym-free biceps

chamber pot

fire pit

eclipse

pond

boxing gloves

bird house

sick bag

sieve

cement mixer

Cauldron

traffic cone

low-interest
savings account

club bag.

chimney

police helmet

fishbowl

earrings

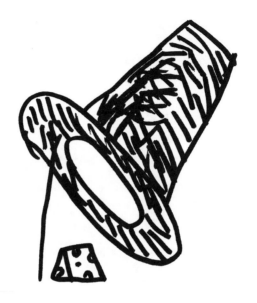

<u>trap</u>

foot spa

exhaust

coracle

conjuror's prop

footrest

trophy

jack-in-the-hat

handbag

jug

discount uggs

package (handed to owner)

loudhailer

<u>umbrella</u>

paint kettle

mug

magazine rack

bell

flea collar

font

dog carrier

coffee table

<u>u r n</u>

L.B.D.

drum

hutch

lamp shade

goblet (of fire)

flowerpot

satellite dish

water butt

ostrich egg cup

<u>hod</u>

ice bucket

gruel bowl

giant's

thimble

fondue

fruit bowl

friend

Family bucket

weights

dog bowl

wicket keeper's
glove

crown

hangover
remedy

cocktail shaker

windsock

coal scuttle

helmet

bird feeder

buttock
enhancement

holster

challenging
art piece

shower cap

plot device

D

NASA

space
shuttle
tip

grail (holy)

punnet

sink

extra pockets

gentlemen's
convenience

mouse bath

petrol can
(not recommended)

pint glass

Popcorn bucket

Snooker Pocket

Method for deciding whether children are good or evil

<u>weapon</u>

patriotic headwear

ALLAN JENKINS is the award-winning editor of *Observer Food Monthly*. He was previously editor of the *Observer Magazine*, and once lived in an experimental eco-community on Anglesey, growing organic food on the edge of the Irish Sea. He lives in north-west London.

Praise for *Plot 29*:

'Like Helen Macdonald's *H Is for Hawk*, this is a profoundly moving account of mental trauma told through the author's encounters with nature ... This is, among other things, a brilliant and brave book about the psychology of gardening'   *Guardian*

'A compelling read ... Jenkins' story raises many questions, not least that of whether it's possible to transcend one's past. After his own agony, is redemption possible? Read this brilliant book, and weep'   *Herald*

'An absolutely original book. Absolutely brilliant. The best family memoir I've read in years'   BILL BUFORD

'Jenkins wrestles the demons from his childhood by planting seeds and helping them grow. He can't overcome the trauma he suffered as a child, but his story is one of courage, resilience, and ultimately, redemption'   *Evening Standard*

'A thoughtful and beautifully realised meditation on families and all the love, loss, pain, healing and regeneration they can bring in their wake. A remarkable achievement' WILLIAM DALRYMPLE

'Jenkins would have undoubtedly written an engaging and fine gardening book but has instead delivered a haunting memoir that will live long in the memory'
Mail on Sunday

'The pacing of the contrasted sections is expertly judged ... *Plot 29* is ultimately a triumphant story of how to learn to love, starting with plants'
Times Literary Supplement

'Brave, exquisitely written and utterly compelling'
NIGEL SLATER

ALSO BY ALLAN JENKINS

Morning: How to make time: A manifesto